# Echoes from the Past

# Echoes from the Past

A pictorial history of the social changes that grew out of the struggle for birth control, and of new threats against this basic human right

Gina Johnson
Johanna Pugni

Blanche Horowitz,
Researcher

Library of Congress
Catalog Card Number: 79-90484

ISBN: 0-934586-03-9

# Contents

# Introduction

The millions who use contraception today are largely unaware of the struggle that secured their right to control their reproduction as they choose. And yet it was recently, in the span of history, that birth control gained popular usage. The battle to win that right lasted nearly a quarter of a century, and is now nearly forgotten.

In the early 1900s, babies were born at home. Margaret Sanger, a nurse whose insights were gained on many confinement cases, witnessed the irrevocable linkage of poverty and poor health to large families then common. Her own mother went through 18 pregnancies and died at the age of 40. Her awareness that having more information about basic biology would help people take control of their lives led her into a life-long crusade.

The advantages of family limitation that Sanger advanced were decried by many religious and civic institutions. She was arrested and jailed for advocating something contrary to custom. Laws prevented her from publishing physiological facts, and from mailing contraceptive information. Bureaucratic authorities denied her the use of public halls. Her offices were vandalized, records stolen or destroyed. She was denounced by anti-feminists, and occasionally ridiculed by the press.

But she was convinced that when individuals gained control over their reproductive capacities, human development would truly be liberated. She persisted in her fight to provide basic information, to challenge bad laws, and to suggest new interpretation of religious doctrine. She waged a courageous battle against prejudice and tradition.

Sanger's efforts gradually won adherents and in time her cause won popular support. Today, birth control has moved into the mainstream of American life. Yet scrutiny of current affairs reveals remarkable similarities between certain conditions then and now. As we near the next century we realize that contraceptive technology has not advanced as far as medical science in general, and though reproductive rights have been won, the ability to exercise these rights is still denied to millions of Americans. Indeed, many of the arguments used then to oppose the individual right to choose are still being voiced. And tragically, incidents of repression and terrorism still occur.

In many ways it appears that difficult lessons of the past are lost and bitter history tends to repeat itself.

# How It Was

---

Steps of stairs. That's how brothers and sisters were often described around the turn of the century. Families were large then, though more so among the poor than the middle or upper classes. In one tenement of 53 families in New York, the census taker found 170 children under 10 years of age. One pregnancy followed upon another. Many young mothers died in childbirth. Those who survived 11, 12 or 13 pregnancies often developed chronic ailments and many died before their 40th birthday. Miscarriages were frequent. Babies died in infancy. Seven or eight living children was an average family.

To support large families, poor parents worked seven days a week in sweatshops, and whole families did piece work at home making shirts, pants, neckties, calico wrappers, underwear, and even cigars and paper bags. Earnings for a twelve-hour day ranged from 25 cents to one dollar. Many worked from daybreak until nine at night, with no time out for meals. But the staple diet of dry bread and coffee was adapted to eating while working.

Boys might escape to the street and live on their own. But work was the only option for girls and most started before they reached their teens. Some pulled threads in factories for 30 cents a day. Modish cashiers in shops commanded two dollars a day, though this was often severely reduced by fines for such violations as 'not being busy' or sitting down. Support of families often depended on women of all ages, who had to accept whatever wages were offered because unions refused to admit them. To lose a day's work was unthinkable, and pregnancy—or even the possibility of it—was a constant threat.

Yet pregnancy was a chronic condition. Remedies to keep from having another baby were wildly sought. Herb teas, steam baths and other nostrums were tried, and even rolling down stairs was resorted to. Failure of all this was evident in the Saturday night lines of 50 to 100 women outside the office of a five-dollar illegal abortionist. They were the lucky ones. Few could afford five dollars. Most tried knitting needles and shoe hooks. It was estimated that some 25,000 women died from the resulting complications each year.

2

"Cheap childhood is
the inevitable result of
chance parenthood."

—Margaret Sanger

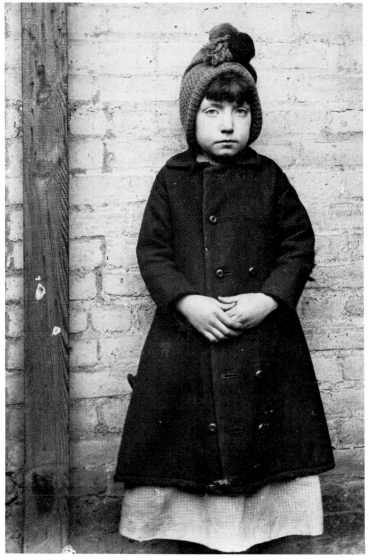

3

4

5

6

7

9

10

11

12

13

14

15

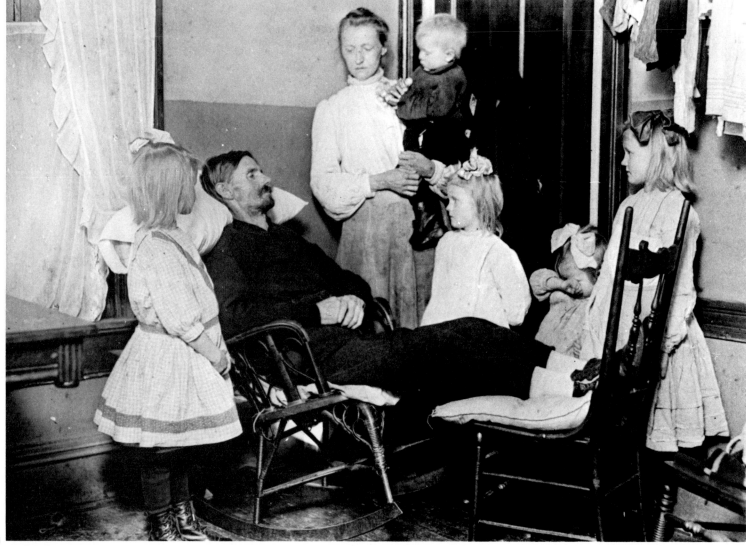

17

18

# Champion of Choice

Preventing conception would provide relief from constant pregnancy. But how? Getting that information and making it available to all the piteous women who begged for it became an obsession with a visiting nurse in the teeming tenements of New York's Lower East Side. Margaret Sanger saw the desperate circumstances of large families living in poverty. Finally one heartbreaking case changed her life.

A young mother suffering from blood poisoning after a botched abortion was Margaret's patient. When Sadie had been nursed back to health she beseeched the doctor for the 'secret.' He laughed and said, "Tell Jake to sleep on the roof." A few months later Margaret was called there again. This time Sadie died within minutes. That incident set the direction of Margaret's entire life.

She recognized that for women to be able to make choices about their lives they must be able to control their reproductive capacities. Sanger began her crusade to obtain factual information on family limitation. There was not much information, but she was convinced that even a little could save lives. Reacting to conditions already existing, and interacting with other forces of change beginning to gather momentum, she began to work aggressively to help the poor with what she saw as their greatest hope—the means to prevent the incessant births that drained mothers physically and fathers financially. Inspired by the importance of this pioneering idea, she called it "birth control."

She was arrested under a federal postal statute that declared contraceptive information obscene and illegal. Later she was arrested for operating a family planning clinic and charged with maintaining a public nuisance. She turned to feminists, suffragettes and trade unionists, hoping they would see the importance of family limitation to their causes. She contacted influential people in medicine, law, politics and society. One spring she toured the country to deliver a major birth control speech 119 times. Clinics seemed to sprout in her wake. She wrote pamphlets, articles and books. She helped found the National Birth Control League, the first birth control organization in America. She arranged international conferences. And she agitated for changes in state and federal laws.

In those early days, a few men supported the movement, but most of the pioneers were women. Their courageous acts gave impetus to the movement at considerable expense to themselves. Margaret's sister, Ethel Byrne, also a nurse, and another woman, Fania Mindell, helped her open the first clinic and were brought to trial, too. While in prison Ethel went on a hunger strike that achieved a great deal of publicity. She almost died of starvation. When Sanger began publication of a more factual journal, Birth Control Review, Kitty Marion sold it on the streets and was taunted by small boys, lectured by elderly women and harried by policemen asking for her license, though none was needed. Anne Kennedy came from California to help boost circulation of the Review. Socialite Frances Ackermann served for years as treasurer. Marie Stopes, who had established the first birth control clinic in London, rallied many English dignitaries to express publicly their endorsement of Sanger's work before her trial. Feminist Henrietta Rodman arranged meetings to support Margaret's defense. All these efforts were needed because interference continued from several quarters for the next 20 years.

23

"My preparation as a
nurse awoke me to the
sorrows of women."

—Margaret Sanger

25

26

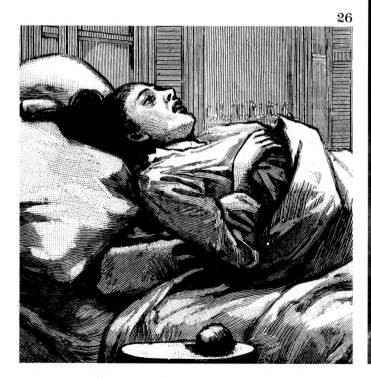

27

Margaret Sanger with Grant (left) and Stuart

Margaret Sanger (center) with Anne Kennedy and Dr. Dorothy Booker of the National Birth Control League 1923

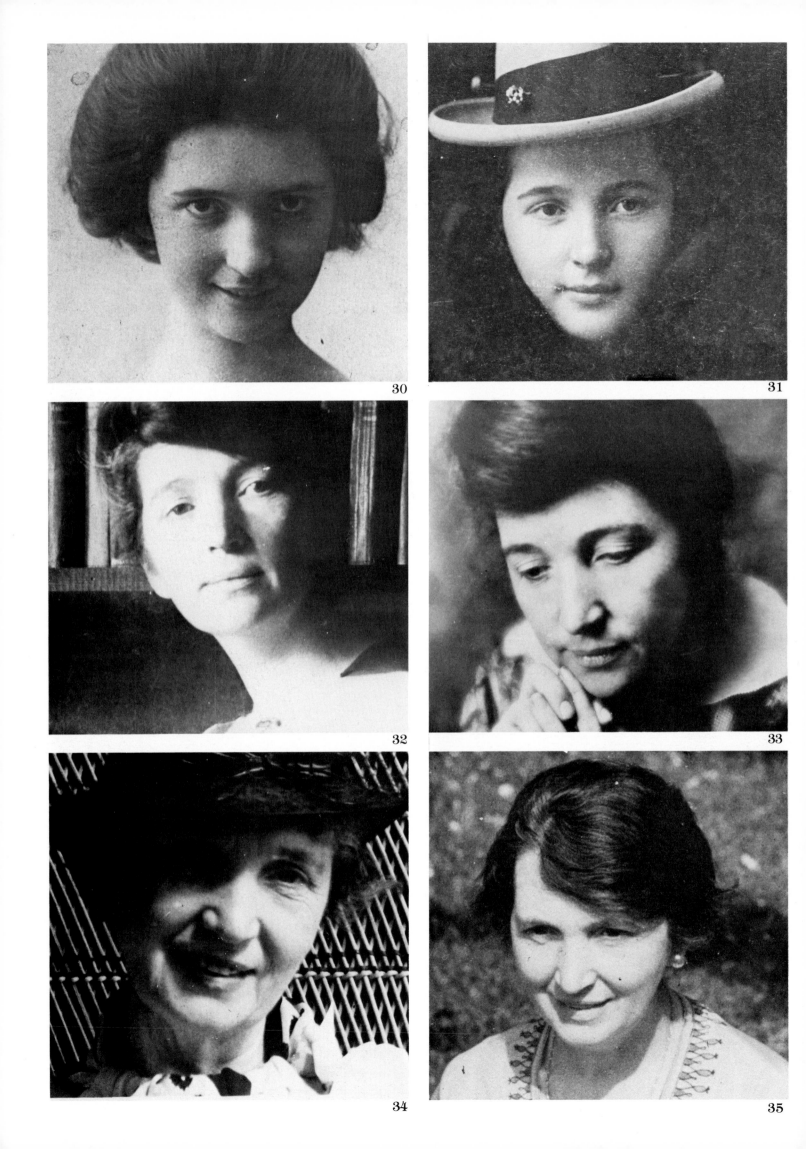

30

31

32

33

34

35

37

# Journey to Freedom

Sanger's first magazine venture, The Woman Rebel, triggered what would be a twenty year battle for legalization of information concerning the practice of birth control. Her most formidable enemy was a group of federal statutes passed around 1873 and popularly known as The Comstock Law. These had been pushed through at the insistence of Anthony Comstock, founder of the New York Society for the Suppression of Vice. This section of the criminal code explicitly banned the mailing, interstate transportation, or importation of "any obscene, lewd, or lascivious or any filthy book, pamphlet, . . . or any drug, medicine, article, or thing . . . intended for preventing conception . . ." The first issue of the Rebel was banned from the mails, other issues were confiscated, and Margaret was faced with a possible prison term of five years and a $5,500 fine. Yet in more than a million letters women continued to plead for specific information. Margaret determined to break down the Comstock wall which kept women in ignorance. She published a pamphlet on "Family Limitation" that described douches, sponges, solutions, and the new diaphragms, with drawings that women could actually understand. When arrested for opening the first U.S. birth control clinic she was imprisoned for 30 days. She continued to publish and was indicted a full nine times, continuing to test the law, despite ongoing opposition from the Society for the Suppression of Vice, The Purity League, and the Patriotic Society. Although Congress and the courts chipped away at repressive obscenity statutes over the years, it was not until 1971 that most of these stringent prohibitions were repealed.

Yet legal opposition was only one of many barriers. The Roman Catholic Church had attacked the birth control movement at its inception. Most of the time the Church confined its opposition to the exercise of its free speech right to oppose pro-birth control legislation. On other occasions, Catholic lay groups and individual clergymen waged open war using less responsible tactics. Father Charles E. Coughlin, the "radio priest," warned that birth control would decimate the "Anglo-Saxons" while allowing numbers of blacks and Polish immigrants to proliferate. Still other Catholic opponents vilified Sanger and her organization, suggesting that she had sinister Bolshevik connections. On one occasion, she was labeled an "enemy and traitor." In 1934, America, a Catholic publication, called for a Congressional investigation of Sanger's National Committee for Federal Legislation on Birth Control. The Knights of Columbus regularly threatened economic reprisals against hotels and meeting halls that rented their facilities to her. On the occasion of the first American Birth Control Conference, some Catholics exploited their political ties to municipal administration to harass birth control advocates. The mayors of Boston, Albany, and the city council of Syracuse, New York, attempted to prevent meetings for discussion of contraception. Archbishop John Gregory Murray of Saint Paul, Minnesota, declared that Catholics in his Archdiocese associated with contraception would be denied the sacraments. The Vatican had given the use of the rhythm method its sanction, but condemned other methods of "unnatural" birth control. In Pope Pius XI Casta Conubii encyclical, the birth control movement was linked to a "new and utterly perverse morality." Those who used birth control "sin against nature and commit a deed which is shameful and intrinsically vicious." Open battle ensued when Archbishop Hayes (later Cardinal) declared war by having the New York City Police Department close down one of Sanger's meetings. It wasn't until the 1930s that the Catholic Church began to accept the futility of such attempts to prevent discussion of contraception.

## THE WOMAN REBEL

### NO GODS NO MASTERS

## NEW WOMAN'S PAPER HELD UP AS OBSCENE

### Uncle Sam Won't Stand for Mrs. Sanger's Remarks on Keeping Families Down.

Deputy Attorney-General W. H. Lamar has declared in Washington that "The Woman Rebel," a monthly paper published in this city, which has just made its initial bow to "an advanced thinking, frankly speaking feminine clientele," is obscene and unmailable at the New York Post-Office or any other post-office. The New York Post-Office was notified of the decision yesterday and acted at once.

In Mr. Lamar's opinion this paper also is incendiary literature. The paper has for its motto:

"No Gods; no masters."

One of the articles is by Mrs. Margaret Sanger of No. 34 Post avenue, who is editor and proprietor of the publication. She deals with what might be termed the voluntary diminishing of the size of families of the poor. She advocates the dissemination of scientific information among poor women and says:

"A law forbids the imparting of information on this subject, the penalty being several years' imprisonment. Is it not time to defy the law? What fitter place could be found than in the pages of the Women Rebel?"

In a leading article it is stated:

"An early feature will be a series of articles written by the editor for girls from fourteen to eighteen years of age. In the present chaos of sex atmosphere it is difficult for the girl of this uncertain age to know what to do or what really constitutes clean living without prudishness."

This article ridicules "white slavery," drugged drink stories and the like, and then declares that it expects to circulate among women of the underworld. These women are asked to voice their opinions in the Woman Rebel and expose police who persecute them.

"A Woman's Duty" is described thus:

"To look the world in the face with a go-to-hell look in the eyes; to have an ideal; to speak and act in defiance of convention."

Woman Rebel claims the right to be lazy; the right to be an unmarried mother; the right to destroy; the right to create; the right to love; the right to live."

Emma Goldman is one of the contributors. Others whose names are signed to articles are Voltairine De Cleyre, Teresa Billington Greig, Dorothy Kelly, Elizabeth Kleen, Catherine Holt, J. Edward Morgan and Marion Howard.

Mrs. Sanger was notified yesterday by Thomas J. Murphy, assistant postmaster, that copies of her paper had been held up at Washington Bridge post-office branch station.

---

ORK CALL—TUESDAY, OCT(

## WOMAN REBEL EDITOR ON TRIAL

### Margaret H. Sanger, Radical Writer, May Be Placed on Trial Today.

Margaret H. Sanger, editor of the Woman Rebel, will be placed on trial today in United States District Court, room 331, Postoffice Building, provided a case begun yesterday is cleared off the calendar. Mrs. Sanger is charged with sending "obscene and indecent" matter through the mail. Simon H. Pollock, her attorney, and many radicals were in the courtroom all of yesterday waiting for the case to be called.

There are four counts in the indictment against Mrs. Sanger. The charges allege "indecency" because of editorial articles written by Mrs. Sanger, in which she is alleged to have advocated birth control.

A strong defense committee is being organized for the purpose of protecting Mrs. Sanger from being railroaded to prison on what is generally considered to be a ridiculous charge.

#### Unjust, Says Mrs. Boissevain.

Mrs. Ines Milholland Boissevain, well known suffragist, when seen by a reporter for The Call yesterday, came out boldly for Mrs. Sanger, saying that a great injustice would be done the defendant should she be convicted.

"This is a question of common sense," said Mrs. Boissevain, who is a lawyer. "A little common sense ought to convince any one that Mrs. Sanger does not come within the meaning of the statute against indecency and obscenity. This statute was intended to make it unlawful to mail pictures without serious purpose, but of a suggestive nature. I refer to the pictures and jokes of the boulevard type.

"But Mrs. Sanger is a serious woman who has certain beliefs on birth control. She bases her ideas on science and biology. What she has written on birth control has been of a serious purpose and not intended in any sense to be filthy. For that

reason it is wrong to say that she has violated the statute. The statute was not drawn up for such a case. This, it appears to me, is plain common sense.

"This case should be brought to the attention of the public. I believe that birth control is a legitimate subject for serious discussion, and for this reason the intelligent women of New York should do something.

#### Plain Talks for Plain People.

"Medical journals discuss birth control. But the writers in these scientific journals couch their ideas in language that is above the head of the average person. It appears as though Mrs. Sanger wrote on the same subject, only she talked plain English that could be understood by plain people, so she has been indicted.

In addition to the charges of "indecency," Mrs. Sanger is alleged to have published a short article which advocated violence. This constitutes the fourth count and will serve to complicate the case, it is said.

Friends of Mrs. Sanger say that the governments of Europe make no effort to suppress discussion of birth control.

---

## WOMAN REBEL'S EDITOR ARRESTED ON P. O. ORDER

### Three Indictments Against Mrs. Sanger—Charge Advocacy of Murder.

Not content with holding up three issues of the Woman Rebel, a monthly journal dedicated to the emancipation of woman, the United States postal authorities yesterday caused Mrs. Margaret H. Sanger, its editor, to be arraigned on three indictments charging violation of postal laws. The authorities allege advocacy of "assassination and the use of dynamite in social reform."

In the two other indictments Mrs. Sanger is charged with publishing "obscene, vile and indecent" articles concerning sex matters. Mrs. Sanger entered a temporary plea of not guilty before United States District Court Judge Hazel, who released her on her own recognizance.

Mrs. Sanger's publication has been censored by the postal authorities, pri-

---

marily at the instigation of Anthony Comstock.

A protest against the refusal to mail the papers was made by the editor and nothing was heard until yesterday. As Mrs. Sanger was at her home, 34 Post avenue, the Bronx, preparing another issue, she was notified by the authorities of the indictments and immediately surrendered herself.

"This had to come sooner or later," she said later, "and I welcome any method of vindicating my theories. Until the postal laws are changed in certain regards, it will be impossible for me to carry out the great work I have started for my sex."

---

## WINS FIGHT FOR BIRTH CONTROL

### Case Against Mrs. Sanger Thrown Out of Court Without a Hearing.

Mrs. Margaret Sanger is not to be tried by the United States Government on the indictment found against her in August, 1914, for sending information about birth control through the mails.

Assistant Federal Attorney Content obtained dismissal of the indictment by Judge Dayton, to the surprise of Mrs. Sanger, who had insistently demanded opportunity to vindicate herself and her cause in court.

Mr. Content presented a memorandum signed by District-Attorney Marshall, which stated that Mrs. Sanger was not a disorderly person, and while the Government believed the magazine articles in question unmailable, there was a reasonable doubt. Besides, for two years she had made no attempt to repeat the alleged offense.

On the strength of these arguments Judge Dayton quashed the indictments. Mrs. Sanger then found herself in the peculiar position of having escaped so much as a trial for writing and sending through the mails literature that caused her husband, William Sanger, to be sentenced to thirty days in jail for the simple act of handing one of the offending documents to a visitor at his office.

Mrs. Sanger, informed that the proceedings had been dropped, called the outcome "a splendid triumph."

Miss Helen Todd telephoned the newspapers that the Sanger Committee, organized for the defense of the accused woman, would hold a jubilation meeting in the Bandbox Theatre to-morrow night.

"We regard the Government's action as a complete vindication," she said. "Mrs. Sanger will speak on.

Anthony Comstock: "Arrest them all. The laws of decency
must be respected."

41

42

"Countless women still die before their time because the
bit of knowledge essential to very life is still not theirs."

—Margaret Sanger

43

45

Margaret Sanger (center) with Drs. Elizabeth Pissoort and Dr. Hannah Stone and nurses after their arrest at the Clinical Research Bureau in April of 1929 when all the case histories of patients were confiscated.

Mrs. Thomas Hepburn, H.G. Wells and Margaret Sanger

46

Addressing a Senate sub-committee during an attempt to remove federal restrictions on the dissemination of birth control information. 1946

When the mayor of Boston threatened to revoke the license of any hall that let her speak, Margaret Sanger appeared in Ford Hall Forum with a large piece of tape across her mouth as her speech was read by someone else.

# Breakthrough

In a move that marked the distance the birth control movement had progressed since 1914, Sanger organized the National Committee for Federal Legislation for Birth Control in 1929. Its task was elephantine—to get the "Doctor's Bill" through Congress. The goal—to open up the mails to birth control information and materials sent by doctors, hospitals, or druggists for the care of patients. Campaign efforts were backbreaking, yet the bill failed again and again. But monumental efforts were not wasted. The long campaign awakened millions to the need for reform. Scientific bodies began to favor birth control; in 1931, the New York Academy of Medicine demanded that Federal and State laws allow doctors complete freedom to impart contraceptive information. Public opinion was staunch; by 1936, a Fortune magazine survey showed that two out of three Americans favored availability of birth control information to all. In 1935, the country was deep in depression. Twenty-two million people were on the federal relief rolls; over 14 million workers were unemployed; half the nation's births were in families on relief struggling desperately to survive on less than $1,000 per year. The climate was ripe for social change; hopefully, the courts would be sensitive to reform and alleviation of misery and dire poverty suffered by millions. It was time for action.

Sanger decided to attack in what was to be one of the most significant cases of the movement—the "One Package" case. She arranged for samples of a new Japanese pessary to be sent to her office in New York. The package was seized by customs agents. She then arranged for a Japanese doctor to send another package to her colleague, Dr. Hannah Stone. Again the package was confiscated by customs agents. Here was a chance to challenge the law and its interference with the free flow of information within the medical profession. The case came to trial in December, 1935. The court ordered the Collector of Customs to deliver the package to Dr. Stone. The government appealed to a higher court; in November, 1936, Judge Augustus N. Hand upheld the previous decision. Here was a crowning triumph. In effect, the decision gave physicians the right to import contraceptive materials . . . and it opened up the mails to all materials and literature to and from doctors and other qualified persons. The law's teeth had been pulled. In Margaret's words, it was "the close of one epoch and the dawn of another."

The "One Package" victory made possible the establishment of over 600 birth control clinics in the United States in the early 1940s. Within a few years, the Planned Parenthood Federation emerged, the successor to Sanger's American Birth Control League. One of its tasks was to address itself to persuading the Federal and State government to include birth control in their public health programs. Even though the "One Package" deal had dissipated the cloud of illegality, government moved with painstaking slowness. In 1942, the Chief of the Division of Industrial Hygiene told the Federation:

"There should be a policy of child spacing for women in industries, under medical supervision. In our future visits to the various States this matter will be brought to the attention of the State Health Officers and the industrial hygiene physicians, emphasizing the importance of this phase of conversation to the health of young women, and suggesting that for any further information they write to you directly."

Signatures of 80,000 people in Massachusetts being carried up the State House steps petitioning amendment to allow physicians to prescribe contraceptives. 1966

The government thus had "taken over the job of birth control" fulfilling one of Sanger's long-desired dreams. Barriers continued to fall. One of the most significant breakthroughs occurred in 1958—lifting the ban on contraceptive prescription in New York's municipal hospitals. The victory ushered in a public policy appropriate to a pluralistic society under which Catholic patients and professionals would be free to follow their Church's teachings but would be precluded from preventing non-Catholics from following their own consciences. By the early 1960s, birth control had come of age; it had won a substantial measure of social and official acceptance. The end of the "Comstock Era" was also reached. Restrictions were removed; positive legislation authorized family planning programs. Contraception became legal in all states.

Two influences of the 1960s had far-reaching effects. On the medical front, research on oral contraception was undertaken in the search for a simpler, more effective method. Even after her retirement, Margaret Sanger was instrumental in getting funding from wealthy friends. The birth control pill was developed through the efforts of Dr. Gregory Pincus and his associates. A few years later, an estimated one of every six women of childbearing age in the United States had adopted this method.

At the same time striking changes in population patterns began to register. The 1960 census showed that the number of people in the United States had nearly trebled since the beginning of the 20th century. Birth rates had been falling over that period, but life expectancy had been greatly extended. Concerns about consumption of resources and other population pressures reached grave proportions. There was popular emphasis on 'replacement' families (two children replacing parents), and the importance of stabilizing population growth. Whether due to this or other causes, the average number of children American couples felt desirable was 2.5, far below the family size of 50 years before.

One of the most formidable hurdles that remained was the legalization of abortion. A trend toward liberalization began in 1967 when Colorado relaxed its abortion statute. Subsequently, 16 other states either liberalized or repealed anti-abortion laws. In January 1973, the U.S. Supreme Court, by a 7-2 vote in two landmark decisions, declared abortion lawful in all states. Legal abortion was, and remains, a most sensitive issue. Controversy over social and moral implications continues today, and the reverberations will probably continue into the future.

56

57

58

59

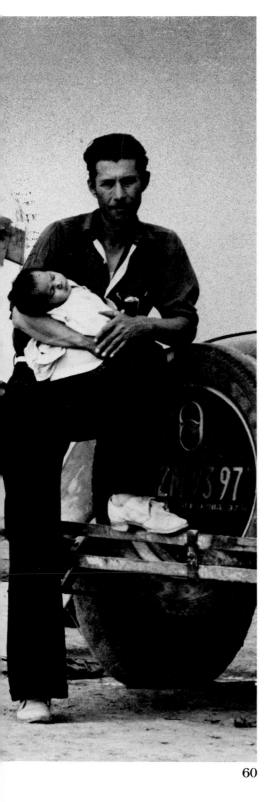

60

61

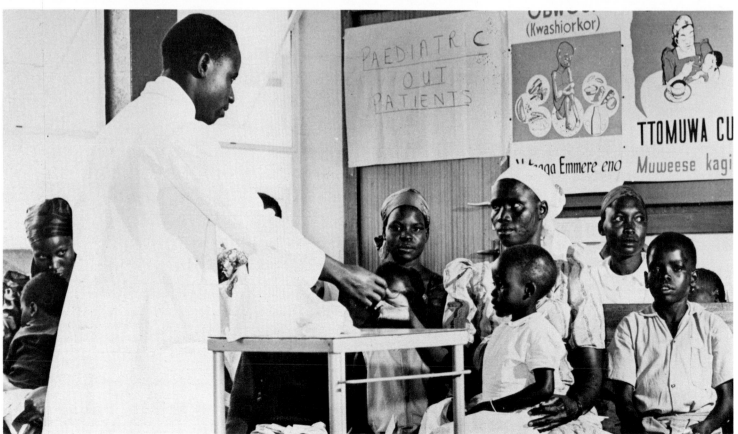

# SHE NEVER CHANGES...

# BUT THE REST OF THE WORLD DOES!

In 1924 when Orphan Annie was born, there were 106,021,000 of us. In 1999 when she and her dress are 75 and we've multiplied to 362,000,000; will there be no room left for her, Sandy...or us?

**THE INDIVIDUAL & THE POPULATION DILEMMA CONFERENCE • March 29-30 • Pierson Hall • UMKC**

Statement signed by **172** Nobel Prize winners asks United Nations to act on population explosion. 1960

Gregory Pincus, M.D.

John Rock, M.D.

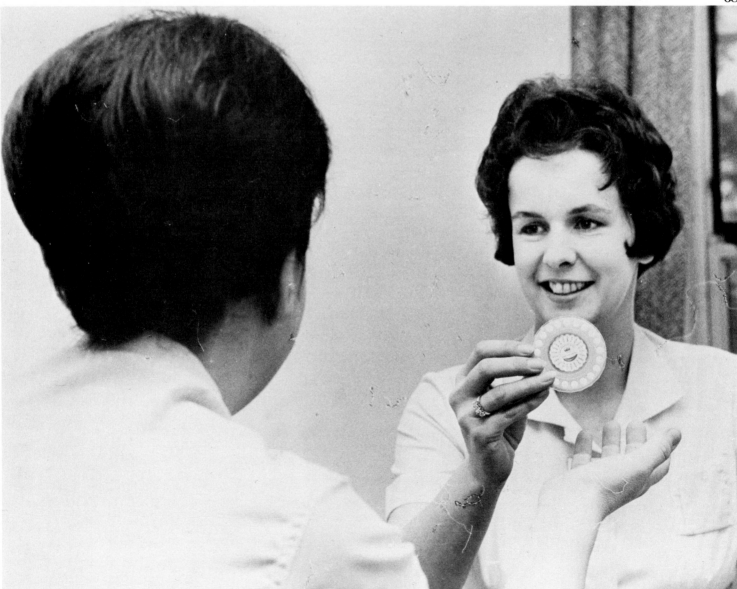

"Life has taught
me we must put
our convictions
into action."
—Margaret Sanger

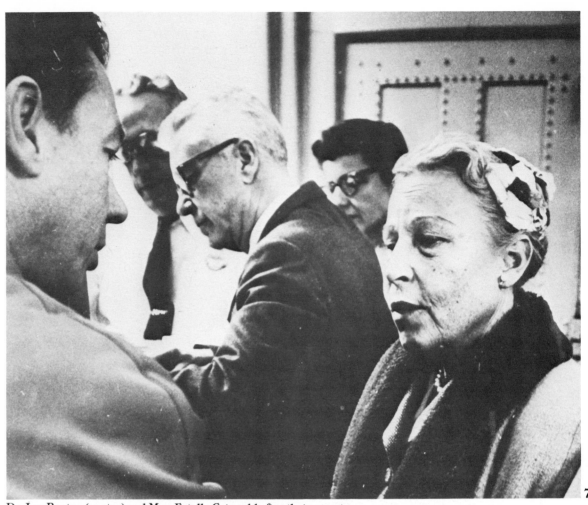

Dr. Lee Buxton (center) and Mrs. Estelle Griswold after their arrest
for violation of old Connecticut anti-birth control law. 1961

Illinois Public Aid Commission votes state-financed birth control for welfare families. 1962

76

77

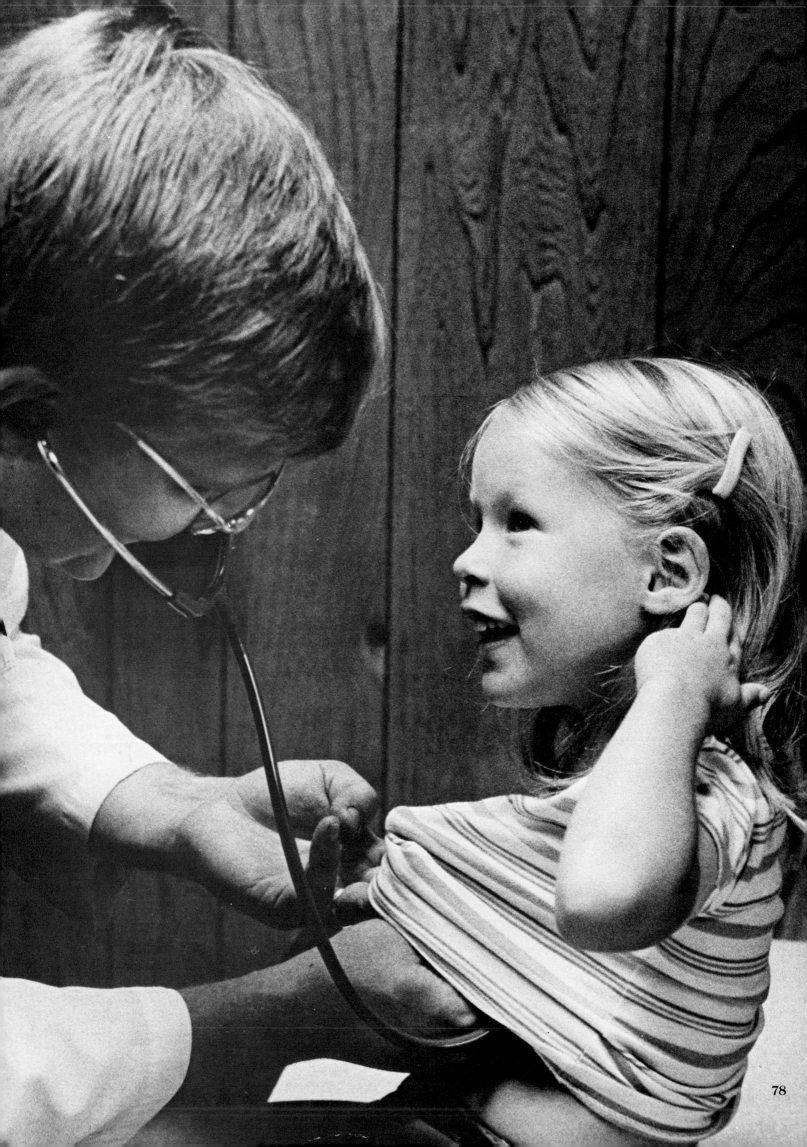

# A Happier Heritage

That the benefits of birth control constitute a constructive force economically and socially is indisputable. Shortly after the turn of the century, Queen Wilhelmina of the Netherlands awarded a royal charter and a medal of honor to the league operating birth control clinics. That country reported the lowest rate of mothers' deaths, while the United States had one of the highest. Further, the infant death rate in the three Dutch cities with the most active clinics was the lowest in the world.

In addition, as early as 1865, it was noted that women bearing many children incurred increased health risks, as did their children. Since then, worldwide experience and the compilation of numerous studies indicate that family planning favorably influences the health, development, and well-being of families and individual members in a myriad of ways: lowering levels of fetal, infant and childhood mortality and sickness; improving the physical, mental and intellectual development of children; securing the health and life of the mother; enhancing family health en toto; and making it possible for women to have children at the ages at which pregnancy carries the least risk.

While family planning was a boon to all women, it meant virtual survival to those who needed it most—needy women and men living on marginal incomes. As Planned Parenthood's clinics radiated across the country, the poor were able to receive quality medical care at low or no cost. Planned Parenthood affiliates operated clinics in more than 700 separate locations in 42 states and the District of Columbia. By 1978, over 1.2 million people, the majority medically indigent, were served in those centers.

But the Planned Parenthood of today has expanded its horizons considerably. For all clients, family planning help means much more than birth control. It is one of the most important "entry-points" into the nation's health care delivery system. Many low-income clients, who comprise 75 percent of the total caseload, receive their first pelvic examination, their first breast examination, their first tests for cervical cancer and, when indicated, testing for sexually transmitted diseases at a Planned Parenthood center. Stretching the comprehensive reproductive health care umbrella even further, the organization serves as the nation's largest single source of referral for women seeking guidance with problem pregnancies; where community need is great some programs offer prenatal care.

In human terms, on a personal level, no single contribution—educational, legal, economic—has served so significantly to secure for women true sovereignty over their lives. And helping people plan their families contributes to a more happy, healthy and loving environment for children. Many by-products of family planning—a sense of being in control of circumstances and able to make future plans—are reflected daily in the enhanced quality of people's lives.

Today's families have options that were unheard of a mere century ago. Today's couples can plan when and whether they will have children. Today's couples are better able to secure for themselves and their children financial security, educational and career goals—futures of fulfillment and achievement.

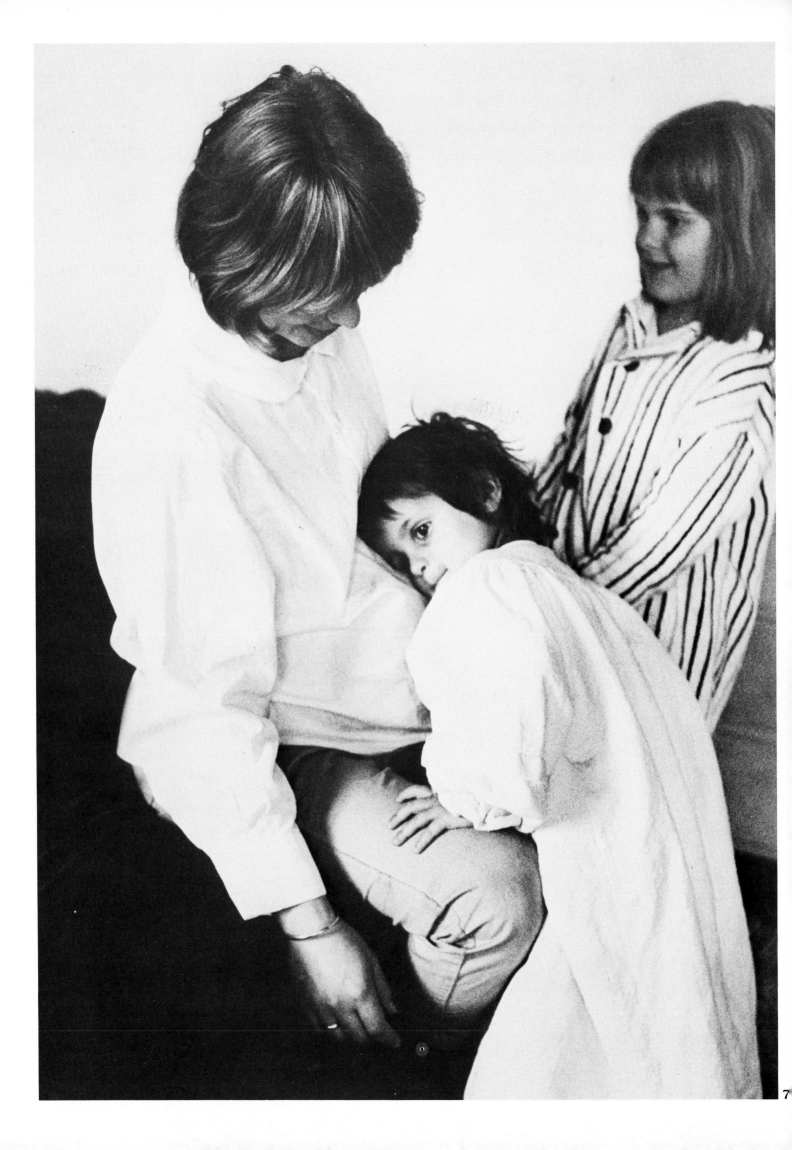

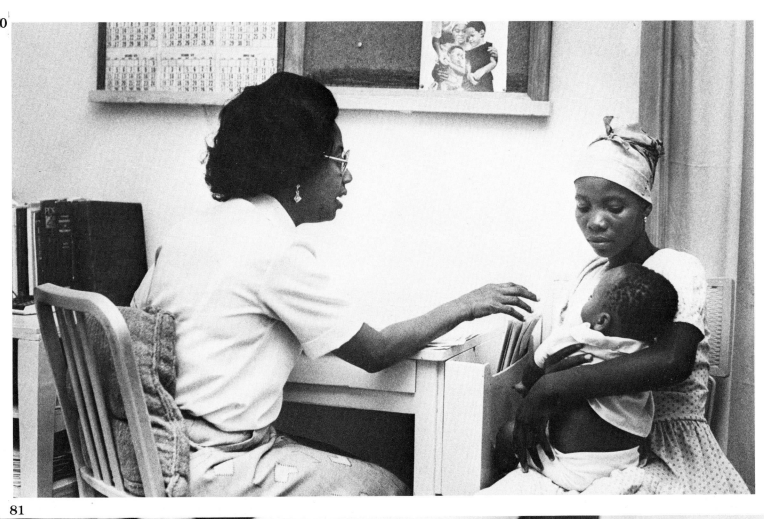

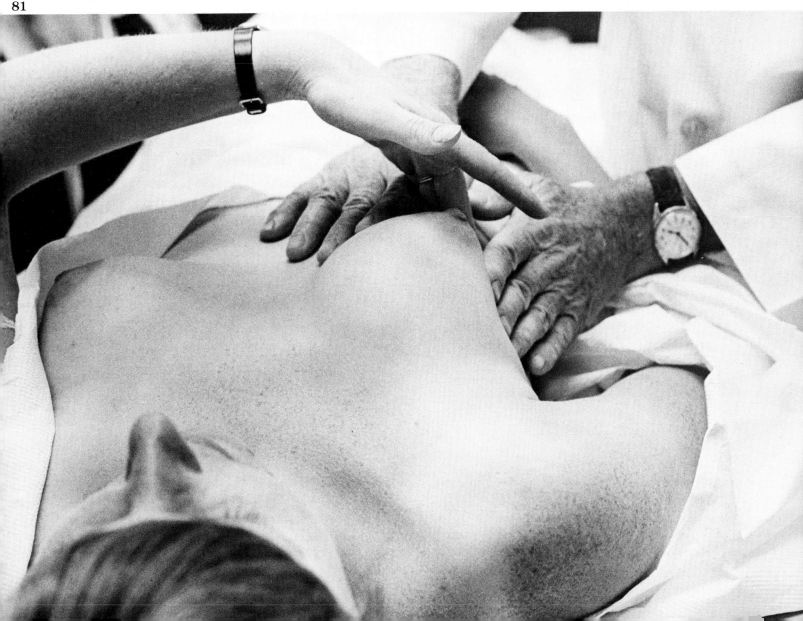

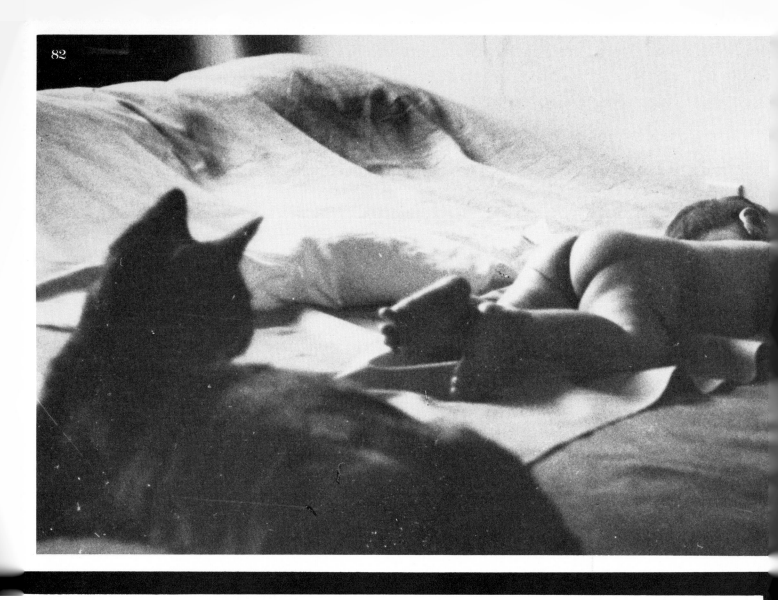

86

"The welfare of
a country is the
quality of its
human beings."
— Margaret Sanger

87

89

90

91

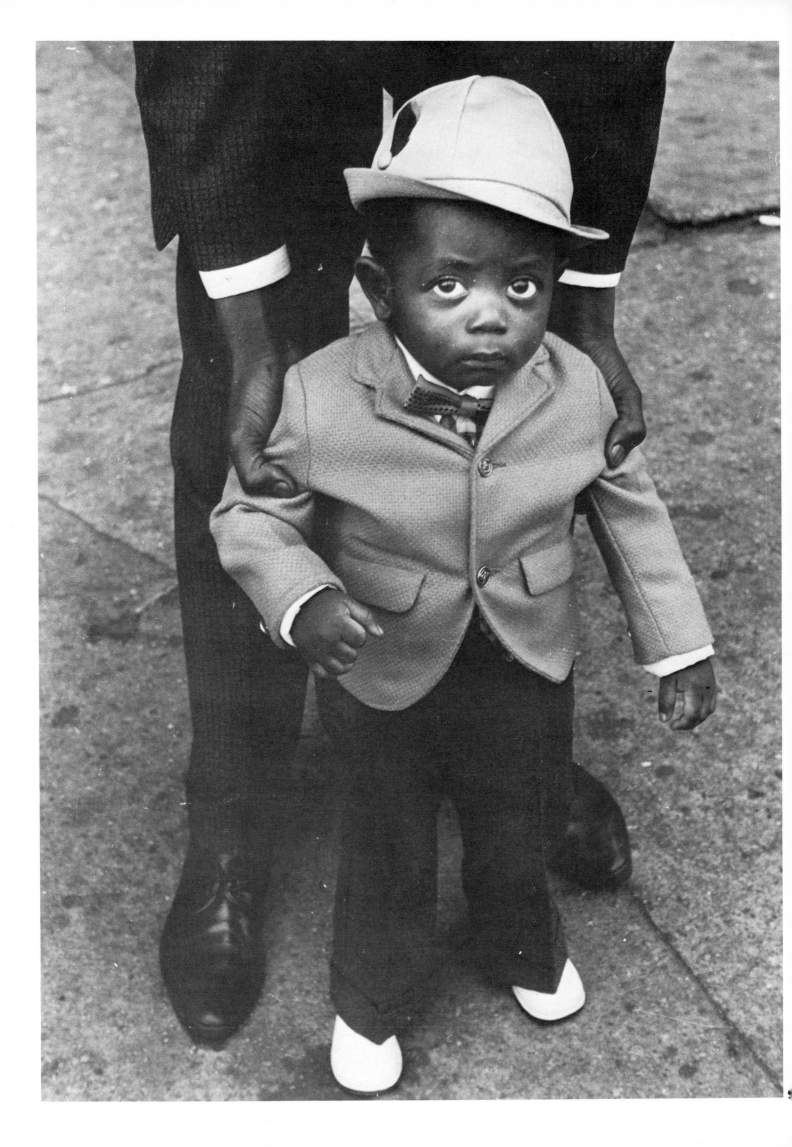

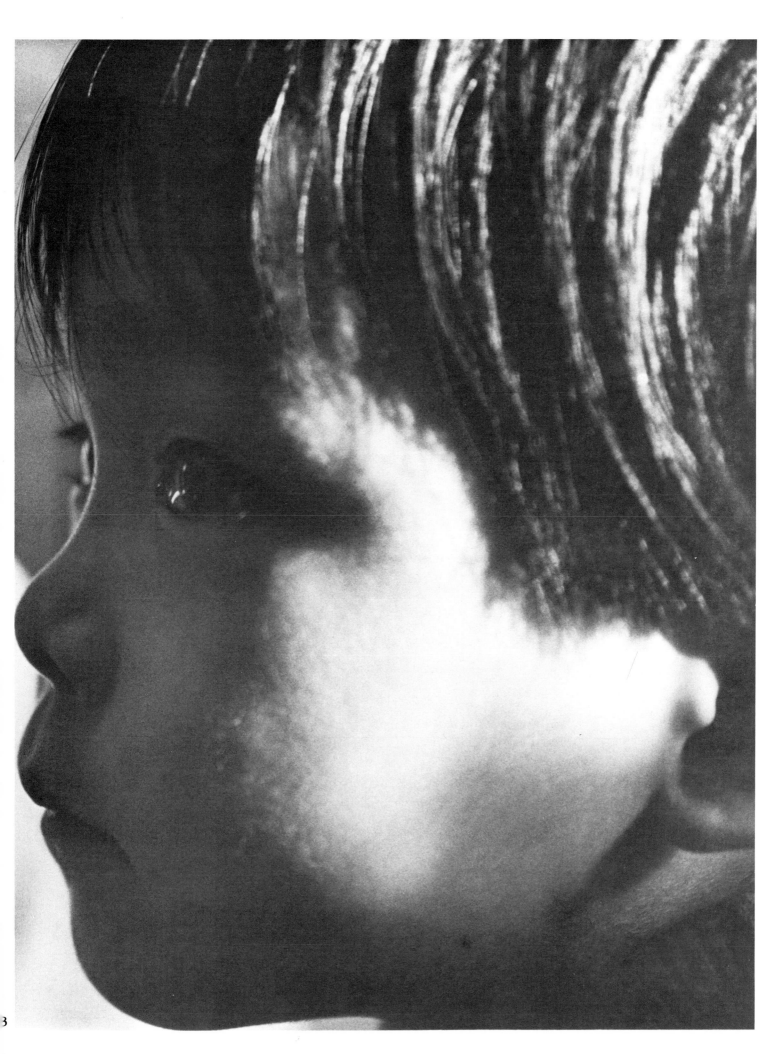

94

95

"Birth control:
two short words answer the
inarticulate demands of
millions of men and women
in all countries."

—Margaret Sanger

98

100

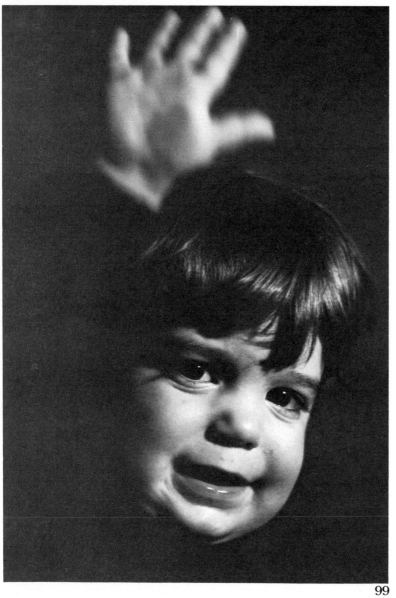

99

101

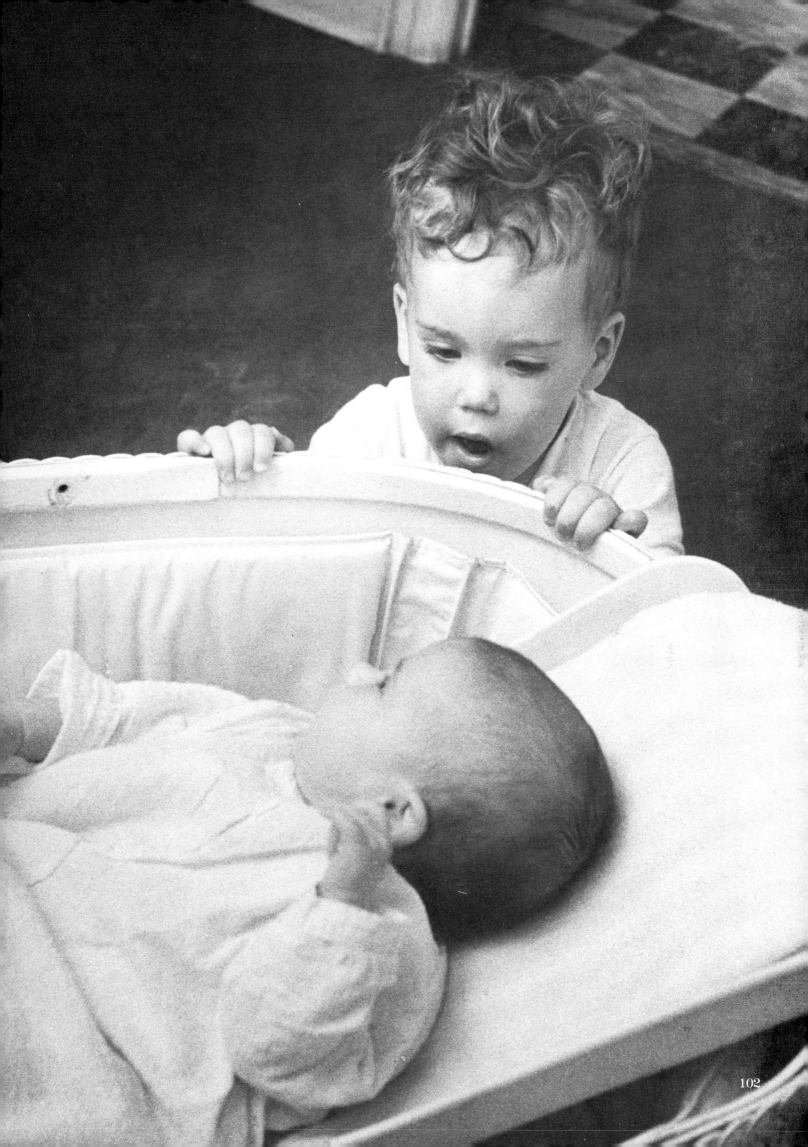

103

104

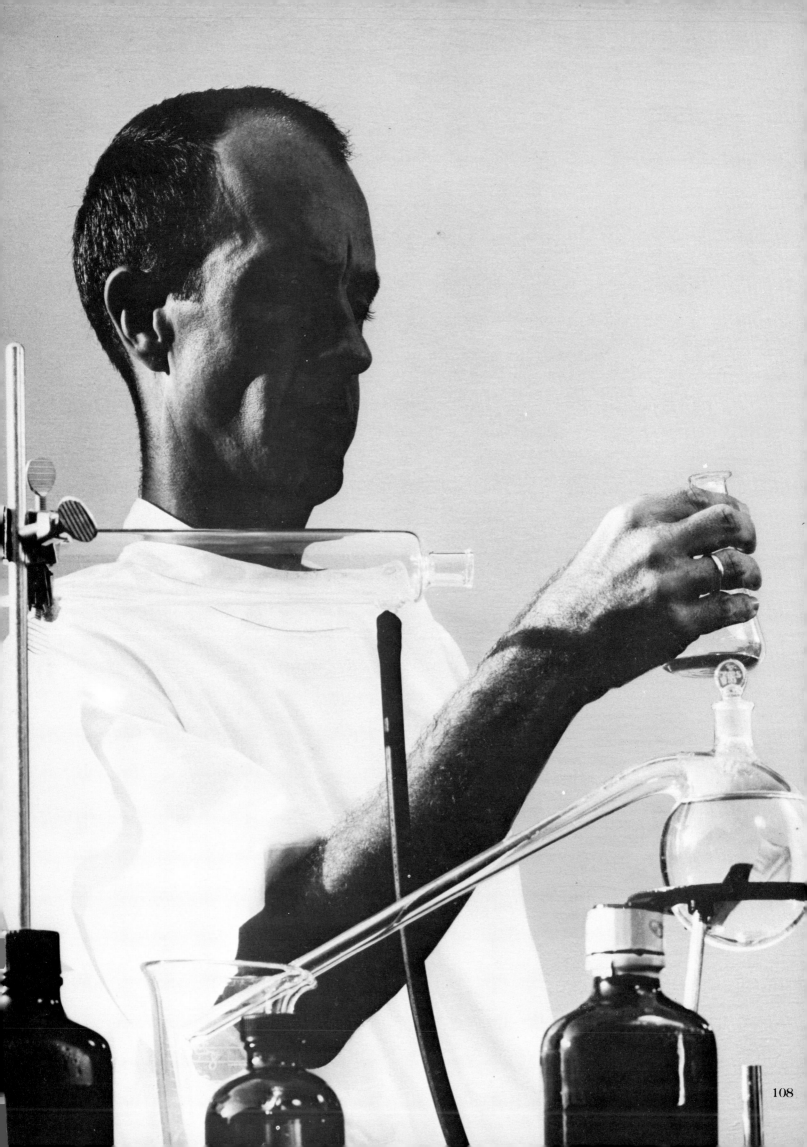

# Anatomy of Change

After advancing by inches, the birth control movement in the 1960s began to take wings. From apathy and hostility, public opinion overwhelmingly endorsed family planning, and changes took place at jet speed. Legislation authorizing family planning programs replaced previous restrictions. More reliable methods, which were easier to use, were introduced, thereby allowing more couples to be successful in having a family the size that they wanted. Public funds were allocated to assist couples with low or marginal income to have access to services. Public health records clearly indicated fewer women suffering the after affects of botched back-alley abortions. Birth control found the broad acceptance that was Margaret Sanger's dream.

The impact was widespread. Where Planned Parenthood centers had been the major providers of services, they were joined by programs in local public health departments, hospitals, and other public and voluntary agencies. Anti-poverty programs incorporated family planning services, as did maternal and infant care programs. Training programs were developed for professionals in the health, education and social services systems. Foundations, research organizations and universities became involved with family planning, and bio-medical and demographic research efforts were launched. The explosion of information triggered enterprises by commercial producers, and the mass media carried scores of favorable articles on the topic that 50 years earlier brought Margaret Sanger to court.

The influx of federal funding was substantial. From almost nothing in 1964, allocations had reached $187 million 10 years later. However, the five-year plan drawn up under the Family Planning Services and Population Research Act, passed by Congress in 1970, languished before completion because of failure of the federal government to increase funding in proportion to the growing demand for services. Still, by the mid-1970s more than four million people needing subsidized service were served by programs receiving federal funding.

110

111

112

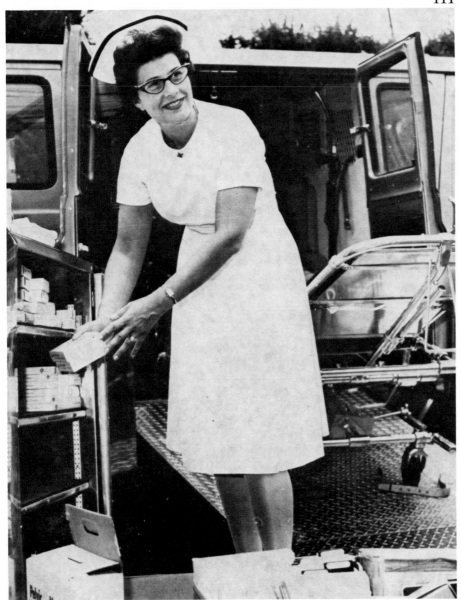

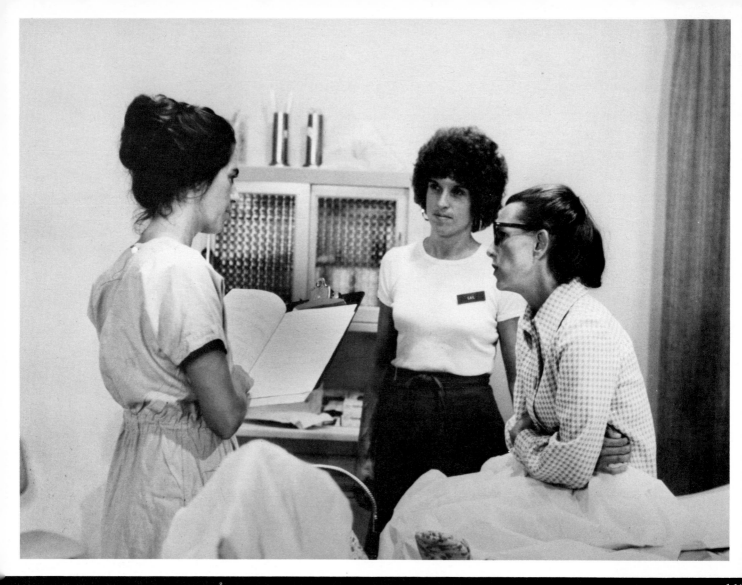

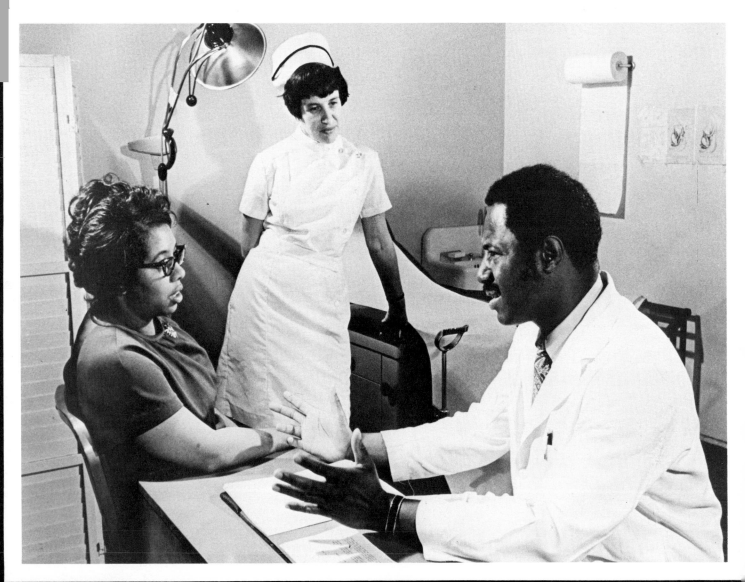

117

"You can almost tell people's age now by their attitude toward birth control."
— Margaret Sanger

1

123

122

Harry Emerson Fosdick congratulated by Edward Lewis, executive director of the Urban League of Greater New York, and Dr. Ira Ferquson of Tuskegee Institute on receiving Lasker Award from Planned Parenthood. 1954

124

125

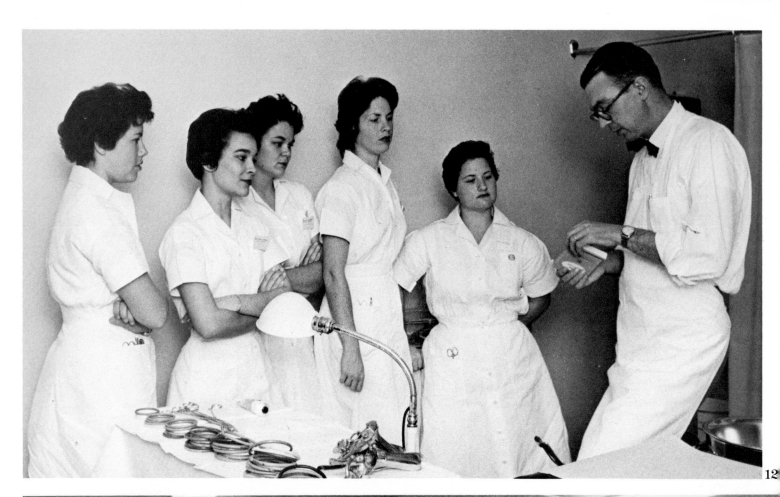

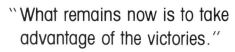
"What remains now is to take
advantage of the victories."
—Margaret Sanger

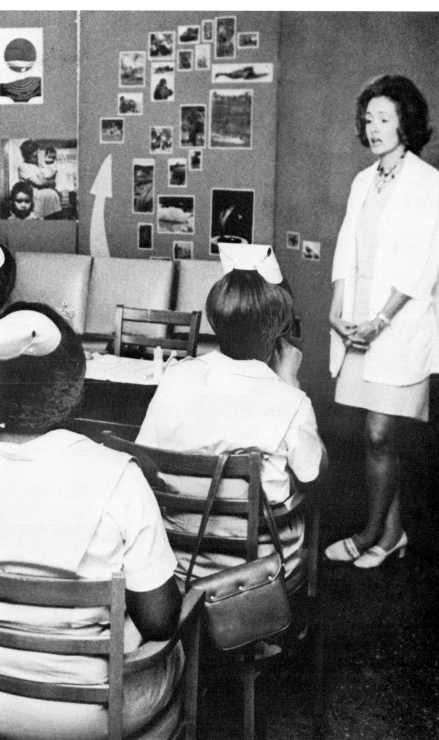

# New Needs Arise

Progress has been substantial. Subsidized family planning programs now operate in all 50 states. Surveys show that nine out of 10 married couples have used or expect to use some form of contraception. Three-quarters of contraceptors use one of the more effective methods. Information on birth control can be given freely. It might seem that Margaret Sanger's dream had become reality. But a closer look reveals that much remains to be done.

Millions of Americans still do not have access to birth control services. This is especially true in small towns and rural communities. But it may also include inner city dwellers whose community hospital does not have a family planning clinic, or whose understanding of the English language or familiarity with the health system pose problems.

Civil and religious activists still oppose freedom of reproductive choice. Though divergent views exist on certain issues, the law protects individual conscience. No one is forced to act against personal belief; just as no one should prevent another from exercising private philosophical or religious practices. That reproductive choice is legal is meaningless unless everyone is free to live according to personal moral and ethical convictions.

Teenagers are a group in particular need of help. Studies reveal that they begin sexual activity earlier than previous generations, some as early as puberty. Yet less than half of the sexually experienced know the basic facts about human reproduction. Sex education programs in many places are superficial, or do not exist at all. As a result, over one million pregnancies occur every year among teenagers with consequent major problems to themselves and society. Teenage pregnancies usually signal curtailed education and a stunted future, a forced marriage or out-of-wedlock parenthood. For very young mothers pregnancy and childbirth pose health hazards for the woman and her child.

The failure rate of contraceptives, and even the failure to use contraception on occasion, indicate that the ideal method still does not exist. It should be safe, of course, with no dangerous side effects. It should be close to 100 percent reliable, yet easily reversible. And something that's simple and easy for the majority of people to use. It shouldn't cost much, and should be distributed widely. Because none that exist meets these criteria there is a pressing need for improved contraceptive technology.

The need for services, information and better technology is multiplied a thousandfold in the less-developed world. In many countries where population growth is rapid, economic development needs are also acute. The financial resources of their hard-pressed governments are inadequate in mounting large scale family planning programs. Yet the people desire these services. Countries with such programs show significant improvement in maternal and child health, and declines in birthrates. Of course, stabilization of population alone will not correct all social and economic problems. But it can ease immediate pressures and provide time to work out long-range solutions.

131

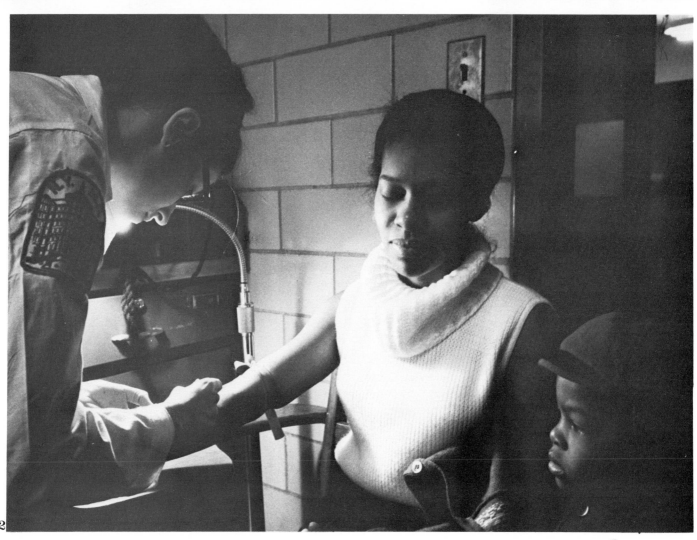

132

``The function
of maternity
overburdens the
capacity of the
girl mother.''
—Margaret Sanger

134

135

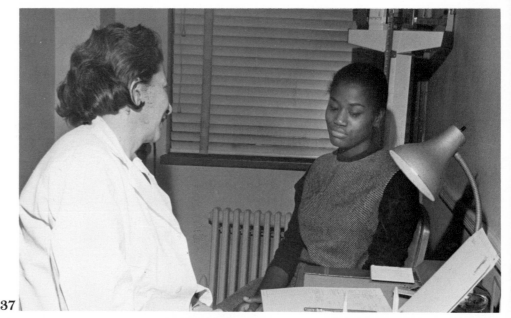

137

138

**Happy Family Planning**
**Feliz Planificación Familiar**
**Un Heureux "Planning" Familial**
السعادة في تنظيم العائلة
快樂的家庭計劃

139

145

"Enforced motherhood
is the most complete
denial of a woman's
right to life and liberty."

—Margaret Sanger

156

157

158

159

ABORTION RIGHTS PROTECT THE ALREADY BORN
EVERY WOMAN'S RIGHT TO CHOOSE!

NO STERILIZATION ABUSE

NATIONAL LAWYERS GUILD

WOMEN FIGHT BA

MY BODY BELONGS

Women STOP THE SEPARATE CHURCH AND STATE

Separate Church & State

DEFEND SAFE & LEGAL ABORTION Now Again! PRO-CHOICE ACTION COMMITTEE

Keep Your Laws Off My Body

My Body My Choice

ABORTION: A WOMAN'S RIGHT

Pro Choice is the Choice

FIGHT THE TERROR of ILLEGAL ABORTION

WOMEN HAVE BECAUSE OF HYDE

REMEMBER Stop the "Pro Life" BOMBERS

KEEP ABORTION SAFE AND LEGAL

Keep Your Laws On My Body

CINCINNATI ABORTION RIGHTS COMMITTEE

160

# Conflicts Remain

The major challenges of developing improved contraceptives, of assuring access to all birth control options, of reducing the incidence of teenage pregnancy, and of assisting less-developed countries require great efforts. These efforts face much the same kind of anti-choice attacks as the early pioneers. Though poll after poll shows that those who oppose the availability of sterilization and abortion or the provision of sex education in the schools are in the minority, the efforts of the vocal few to impose their convictions on the majority are unceasing.

Today's pressure tactics repeat some used decades ago. Sectarian medical institutions threaten to disaffiliate physicians who perform procedures in abortion clinics. Religious societies threaten corporations that contribute to non-profit agencies that provide services or referrals. Individuals boycott businesses that supply materials or rent space to abortion clinics. One scare tactic is to circulate the idea that an abortion clinic lowers the property values in a neighborhood.

Other strategists work within the system. Opponents of abortion petition their representatives in local, state, and federal government to change the law, to encompass it with restrictions, and to deny public funding to subsidize abortion. They work politically to defeat candidates who might favor the right to choose. This can be an effective maneuver in a close election where two percent of the returns can sway the outcome. A single issue vote may be the narrow margin that determines the kind of incumbents an entire community, a whole state or even the nation will have in office.

Rhetoric, of course, is rampant. Street demonstrators carry signs alleging: "Abortion—Crime that Pays," or "Death for Sale." Accusation of "Murderers" are among the more polite terms shouted at clinic personnel. Such general threats escalate into personal ones. People's lives and the lives of their children are threatened. Rocks are thrown through windows of homes, windows are shot out, and paint is splattered on walls.

What starts as picketing often culminates in physical abuse of both staff and clients, attempts to take over clinic waiting rooms, efforts to prevent women from entering clinics or receiving attention, and destructive attacks against clinic records and property.

Such a charged atmosphere invites more serious violence, and it has occurred. Top of the list in terror tactics have been several fire bombings.

The objective of all this, naturally, is to dissuade any further attempt to effect change. Today's birth control activists would betray their predecessors were they to retreat from their belief that the freedom to choose is a basic human right. Against all odds, they will continue to put their convictions into action.

Rev. Beatrice Blair and Rev. Howard Moody place a proclamation denouncing Catholic Church's position on abortion on the door of St. Patrick's Cathedral in New York.

"The rights of women have found voices . . . intermingled with millions of voices demanding freedom."

—Margaret Sanger

"We figure they're safe as long as they don't know what they're doing."

63

64

165

166

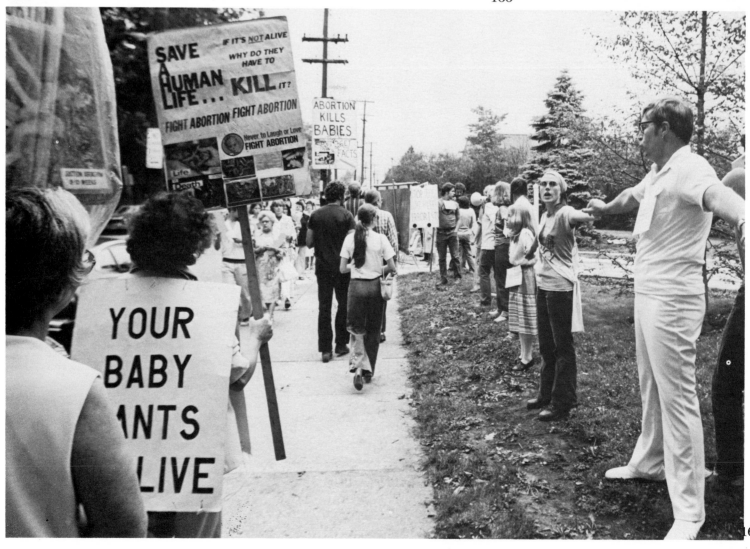

167

**168**

Students from St. Thomas Academy, Derham Hall High School and Visitation Convent picket in front of Planned Parenthood clinic in St. Paul, Minnesota.

169

171

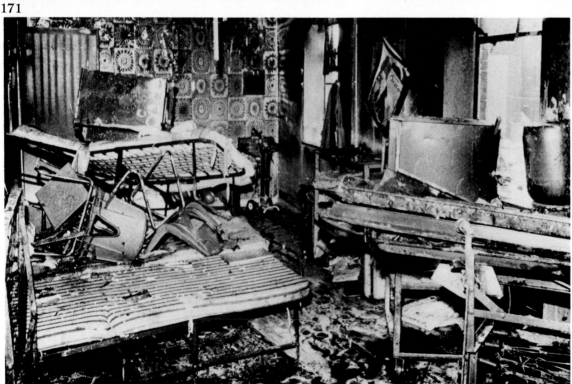

172

170

173

``Enlightenment will be extinguished . . .
unless applied . . . to the machinery of
political and legislative action.''

—Margaret Sanger

# Chronology of the Birth Control Movement

The need of human beings to control their reproduction undoubtedly dates as far back as prehistoric man. The chronology of birth control efforts in recorded history covers many centuries. Contraceptives used thousands of years before Christ are described in ancient Chinese writings and in Egyptian papyrus. The beginning of the modern movement was the publication in 1798 of an Essay on Population by the Reverend Thomas Robert Malthus. This English clergyman and economist was one of the first to stress the importance of balancing the earth's resources with its people. Malthus advocated abstinence, and described dire results were this not practiced.

It is not generally known that a primary role in the development and growth of the idea was played in the United States. Two ardent champions of Malthus were Presidents Thomas Jefferson and James Madison. Robert Dale Owen, United States Senator and also Ambassador to France, advocated the limitation of families, and his book Moral Physiology had international impact. Ralph Waldo Emerson, Robert Ingersoll and others expressed sympathy and understanding of the idea, and the practical treatise Fruits of Philosophy that popularized the concept of family limitation, was written in Boston by an American physician, John Knowlton.

The history of the great events in the development of birth control can be summed up in this list of dates:

**1798:** First edition of Malthus's Essay on Population.

**1823:** A small leaflet setting forth the economic burden of excessively large families described with frank simplicity hygienic methods of preventing undesired pregnancy. It was circulated in Manchester, England, to the married of both sexes. Known as "The Diabolical Handbill," it was generally attributed to Francis Place.

**1830:** New York: Robert Dale Owen published Moral Physiology, advocating scientific and hygienic practice of contraception. Frances Wright made family limitation part of her feminist program.

**1831:** Beginning of decline in birth rate in France, due to artificial contraception. Eleven years later Bishop Bouvier of Le Mans warned the Pope not to prohibit the practice of contraception if the Church would retain its power over the French.

**1833:** Dr. Knowlton published in Boston, Massachusetts, his Fruits of Philosophy, describing contraceptive methods. This book became internationally important in popularizing family limitation.

**1841:** The Oneida Community was founded by John Humphreys Noyes, at Putney, Vermont; later moved to Oneida, New York (1848-1881). Noyes wrote in his annual report: "We are not opposed to procreation. We are opposed to excessive, and, of course, oppressive procreation. . . . We are in favor of intelligent, well-ordered procreation."

**1854:** The Elements of Social Science by Dr. George Drysdale, published in London; the first complete presentation of contraception from the economic, philosophical and medical standpoint did more than any other to awaken public interest.

**1869:** Through the efforts of Anthony Comstock of the Society for the Suppression of Vice, contraception was included in an obscenity law passed by the legislature of New York. During the following years many other states enacted laws of this type.

The Roman Catholic Church abandoned its position that ensoulment took place forty days after conception, making abortion before that time lawful, and declared that life begins at conception.

**1873:** Through Comstock's efforts Congress enacted statutes excluding information about contraception from the United States mails, and declaring such information illegal and obscene.

**1877:** Charles Bradlaugh and Annie Besant distributed 185,000 copies of Dr. Knowlton's Fruits of Philosophy (Boston, 1833) in England. They were exonerated of circulating "indecent" literature. Birth rate in England began to decline. Malthusian League organized.

**1878:** First family planning clinic in the world opened in Amsterdam, Holland, by Dr. Aletta Jacobs. Three years later Nieuw-Malthusiaansche Bond began active work among the poor of Holland; Dr. F. Rutgers a pioneer.

**1912:** Margaret Sanger, a visiting nurse of New York City's East Side wrote and published What Every Mother Should Know. The next year she went with her husband and three children to Europe to search for practical family limitation methods in France, England and Holland. Dr. Abraham Jacobi, in presidential address to American Medical Association, endorsed hygienic prevention of pregnancy.

**1914:** January: Mrs. Sanger announced a public campaign for voluntary fertility control, based on grounds of economics and feminism.

February: First issue of The Woman Rebel published and barred from the mail.

April: "Birth Control" coined to express the purpose and aim of campaign. The first American birth control organization formed.

September: Margaret Sanger arrested and indicted for advocating birth control, under federal statute (See 1873). The case was dropped two years later.

**1916:** First American birth control clinic opened in Brooklyn, New York

Margaret Sanger, Ethel Byrne, and Fania Mindell arrested for opening clinic. Sentenced to Blackwell's Island, Mrs. Byrne began hunger and thirst strike. Released by Governor Whitman at end of eleven days. Kitty Marion and others imprisoned for distributing birth control literature.

**1917:** February: Birth Control Review began publication.

April: Margaret Sanger imprisoned for thirty days, for opening first American birth control clinic. Case appealed.

National Birth Control League formed by a group of society women hoping to change the Comstock Law rather than defy it.

**1918:** Judge Crane of New York Court of Appeals decided in the Sanger Case that legally practicing physicians could give contraceptive advice "for the protection of health and the prevention of disease."

**1919:** Organization in America of Voluntary Parenthood League to repeal federal laws against birth control.

**1921:** First American birth control conference, held in November, in New York City, resulted in founding of the American Birth Control League. Mrs. Sanger and Miss Mary Winsor arrested for attempting to address a mass meeting on birth control at Town Hall Club in New York. Arrests instigated without warrant by the Catholic hierarchy. Incident aroused storms of public protest and gave the movement much publicity.

Mothers Clinic for Constructive Birth Control, London, established by Marie Stopes. A year later a society with the same title formed. Organ: Birth Control News.

Birth control clinic opened under auspices of Malthusian League, London—Walworth Birth Control Centre.

International conference on contraceptive devices in Amsterdam, Holland.

**1922:** Margaret Sanger made world tour for birth control, starting organizations in Honolulu, Japan and China.

**1923:** Birth Control Clinical Research Bureau opened by Sanger in New York. Began series of medical contributions on contraceptive techniques.

First bills to legalize birth control information introduced in Connecticut and New York legislatures.

**1927:** The First World Population Conference organized by Margaret Sanger, President of the American Birth Control League and Secretary of the International Federation of Birth Control Leagues, at Geneva, Switzerland, under the chairmanship of Sir Bernard Mallet, England. Steps taken toward permanent organization (Population Union) for the study of population problems.

**1929:** Birth Control Clinical Research Bureau raided. Dr. Hannah Stone, another physician and three nurses arrested; supplies and confidential records seized. Invasion of the confidential relation between doctor and patient aroused a storm of protest and resulted in strong support from the medical profession and community leaders. Defendants all discharged. Birth control became front page news throughout the country.

**1931:** Margaret Sanger received the American Women's Association Medal, for distinguished achievement, and for qualities of "vision, integrity and valour."

The League of Nations adopted the report of its health committee, at its 18th session, officially recognizing child spacing as a problem of public health.

**1936:** A decision of the U.S. Circuit Court of Appeals for the Second Circuit sustained the ruling of Judge Moscowitz of the District Court the previous January that contraceptives imported for a lawful purpose did not come within the restriction of the federal statutes. The most significant passage of this decision declared the statute's design "was not to prevent the importation, sale or carriage by mail of things which might intelligently be employed by conscientious and competent physicians for the purpose of saving life or promoting the well-being of their patients." A Gallup Poll (American Institute of Public Opinion) indicated 70 percent of those questioned favored the legalizing of contraception.

Margaret Sanger received the Town Hall Club Award, given to the member who had made the greatest contribution "to the enlargement and enrichment of life."

**1939:** The Birth Control Federation of America, Inc., formed by a merger of the American Birth Control League and the Birth Control Clinical Research Bureau.

**1942:** Planned Parenthood Federation of America, Inc., became the new, more comprehensive name of the former Birth Control Federation of America.

**1944:** Consumers' Union received a favorable decision in the United States Court of Appeals of the District of Columbia in its case vs. Frank J. Walker, Postmaster General, which allowed them to mail a pamphlet on contraceptive materials tested, and found effective and non-injurious, to members requesting it.

Dr. Jacob Yerushalmy's study of 7 million births reprinted. The chief statistician in the United States Public Health Service concluded that this country's high stillbirth rate could be lowered by properly spacing the time between births.

**1945:** The Sanger Bureau established a fertility service to help childless couples.

Hannah Stone Planned Parenthood Memorial Center opened in Harlem, New York City, where the stillbirth, infant and maternal mortality rates were three times higher than in any other section of the city.

**1947:** Nationwide poll of American physicians conducted by Dr. Alan F. Guttmacher, showed 97.8 percent favored birth control. He also received a Lasker Award for "conspicuous service toward healthier marriage and parenthood."

520 clergymen asked for Federation material which was used in 4,182 sermons and 152 Family Week addresses.

The Federation cooperated in organizing the first comprehensive research program in the field of human reproduction—to be undertaken by the National Research Council in behalf of the National Committee on Maternal Health working in collaboration with the Planned Parenthood Federation of America.

Six Protestant physicians were dismissed from the staffs of three Roman Catholic hospitals in Connecticut because they refused to withdraw from the "Committee of 100", a group of doctors supporting a pending birth control bill which would permit physicians to give this information to patients whose health would be endangered by pregnancy.

Resolution endorsing aims of Planned Parenthood signed by nearly 4,000 Protestant and Jewish clergy . . . "planned parenthood is one expression of the religious principle that affirms the infinite worth of a human being."

1948: At Cheltenham, England, the International Conference on Population and World Resources in Relation to the Family was held under the auspices of the Family Planning Association, largely as the result of Margaret Sanger's efforts. Mrs. Sanger and Dr. Abraham Stone attended. Important representatives from more than 20 nations attended. It was the largest and most important post-war conference on the family and resulted in formation of the International Planned Parenthood Committee.

1950: Mrs. Margaret Sanger received a special Lasker Award for being "foremost in teaching families wise planning in birth control; leader in influencing nations toward balanced population; living to see her beginning in city slums grow into plans for a planet."

1951: The Worcester Foundation for Experimental Biology, supported in part by Planned Parenthood Federation grants, initiated a lengthy research program under Dr. Gregory Pincus, to develop simpler and more effective contraceptive techniques.

Professionals and officials from 20 foreign countries sought contraceptive aid and information from Planned Parenthood for their own countries.

1952: St. Francis Hospital in Poughkeepsie, N.Y., ordered seven physicians to resign from the Dutchess County League of Planned Parenthood or resign from the hospital. Publicity was nationwide, most of it criticizing the hospital. As a result, the hospital ignored its own ultimatum.

1958: Removal of the longtime regulation in New York City municipal hospitals forbidding discussion of birth control. Months of campaigning by physicians, professional organizations, community groups and many religious leaders led to lifting contraceptive ban in non-sectarian institutions. Settlement of the controversy provided that hospital personnel with religious objections would be excused from prescribing but could not prevent the practices of others. This had far-reaching effects and became the appropriate basis in a pluralistic society for subsequent changes in policy on fertility control, whether in legislation, court decisions or administrative regulation.

1959: Problems of rapidly expanding populations were studied by U.S. Government committees, and recommendations made to President Eisenhower to provide birth control services in U.S. tax-supported hospitals and through public health departments, and to include such assistance in foreign aid programs to countries requesting it.

1960: The Food and Drug Administration approved the sale of oral steroid pills for contraception.

**1961:** Distinguished citizens of nineteen countries, including thirty-eight Nobel Prize winners and 176 other prominent scientists, writers, health experts, educations and political leaders, presented a Statement of Conviction about Over-population to Secretary Dag Hammarskjold urging the United Nations to give leadership in developing programs of population limitation all over the world.

**1962:** First International Conference on IUDs held in New York; led to Cooperative Statistical Program for the Evaluation of Contraceptive Devices, set up by C. Tietze, M.D.

**1963:** The UN Assembly approved a major resolution on Population Growth and Economic Development, proposed by twelve nations . . . by a 69-0 vote.

A method of freezing sperm was proposed.

Information on IUD efficacy and safety permitted general distribution throughout the world.

**1964:** Catholic professionals from twelve countries in Europe and America petitioned Pope Paul VI for a reappraisal of church teachings on birth control as the Ecumenical Council began deliberations on "The Church in the Modern World".

**1965:** The U.S. Supreme Court ruled Connecticut's statute prohibiting the use of birth control violated personal and constitutional rights of marital privacy; ten other states liberalized old laws or enacted new ones of positive family planning policies and providing tax funds for programs.

**1966:** The Department of Health, Education and Welfare outlined an expanded program for all requesting birth control, as part of a mandate contained in President Johnson's Health Message to Congress to improve and support such services in this country.

The last restrictive legislation on birth control was eliminated in Massachusetts, allowing physicians to legally prescribe contraceptives and druggists to publicly sell them.

**1967:** Department of Health, Education and Welfare found that its operating agencies did not place priority on family planning and were uncertain what was expected in that area.

Colorado reformed its abortion law.

Social Security Amendments allotted a small percentage of maternal and child health funds for family planning in first federal effort to provide services.

United Nations Declaration on Population proclaimed family planning a basic human right; Fund for Population Activities was established.

**1968:** President Johnson appointed Committee on Population and Family Planning, which recommended expansion of services, biomedical and behavioral research, and assistance to developing countries.

**1969:** President Nixon appointed a Commission on Population and the American Future; his message to Congress cited problems created by unequal access to contraceptive services because of economic and social barriers. Department of Health, Education and Welfare established National Center for Family Planning Services within Health Services and Mental Health Administration.

Family Planning Perspectives introduced by the Center for Family Planning Program Development, which was set up a year earlier as a technical assistance arm of Planned Parenthood.

1970: Congress passed the Family Planning Services and Population Research Act. $382 million over three years authorized for service and research (first provision for contraceptive research, and first separate authorization for services).

Nation's most liberal abortion laws enacted in New York, Alaska, Hawaii, Washington.

Environmental Education Act passed, with population education one of several program components.

Appearance of commercial cryobanks, freezing human sperm, parallel growing popularity of vasectomy as contraceptive method.

Title X of Public Health Services Act provided main support for family planning service and educational programs, and biomedical and behavioral research in reproduction and contraception. Center for Population Research established.

Earth Day (Environmental Teach-in) urged federal funding for research in all areas that affect population growth and ecological results.

1971: First all-Africa conference on population; International Planned Parenthood one of cooperating agencies.

Formation of "public sector" programs to carry out contraceptive development research, some in collaboration with industry.

1972: Nation's first family planning stamp issued.

U.S. fertility rate dropped to "replacement" level for full six-month period for first time in history.

Eisenstadt V. Baird: U.S. Supreme Court invalidated a Massachusetts statute limiting distribution of contraceptives to married persons as violation of Fourteenth Amendment.

House of Delegates of American Bar Association approved Uniform Abortion Act, intended as model for legislation by states, allowing licensed physicians to perform abortions on request.

1973: U.S. Supreme Court declared abortion lawful in all states. Roe V. Wade/Doe V. Bolton.

Expenses of preventing conception or terminating pregnancy ruled tax deductible by Internal Revenue Service.

1974: Designated World Population Year by UNESCO; World Population Conference held in New York; World Population Plan of Action adopted unanimously at Bucharest Conference, calling for a variety of research activities in fertility regulation as a priority of nations.

**1975:** Vasectomy reversal through microsurgery reported higher success rate than previous techniques.

National Fertility Study found dramatic rise in numbers of contraceptive sterilizations among couples with all the children they wanted.

**1976:** World population reached 4,000,000,000

U.S. Supreme Court held states may not require a minor to have parental consent to obtain contraceptive services from federally subsidized programs. Food and Drug Administration approved Progestasert intrauterine device that released continuous low dose of progesterone directly into uterus.

Planned Parenthood of Central Missouri V. Danforth: U.S. Supreme Court decided states may not constitutionally require a married woman to have her husband's consent for abortion, nor give parents absolute veto over minors seeking abortion.

**1977:** U.S. Supreme Court invalidated New York State ban on advertising and display of contraceptives, and ruled that minors of any age might buy non-prescription contraceptives.

U.S. Supreme Court held that neither federal law nor the Constitution required states to pay Medicaid benefits for abortions not medically necessary; also held that public hospitals do not have to provide non-therapeutic abortions.

**1978:** Select Committee on Population established by House of Representatives to study causes and consequences of U.S. and world population growth. Congress extended Title X for three years; expanded scope of services.

**1979:** U.S. Supreme Court struck down Massachusetts law requiring minors to have consent of both parents before obtaining an abortion.

Congress passed FY 1980 appropriations for Title X, with services receiving $165 million ($20 million above 1979 levels), and adding $6.1 million to research, bringing that total to $78.5 million.

National Advisory Committee for the White House Conference on Families appointed. Four national White House Conferences on Families, to be held in four regions of U.S., projected for June/July 1980.

# Margaret Sanger: A Selected Bibliography

Margaret Sanger as author.*

Sanger, Margaret. An autobiography. With a new preface by Alan F. Guttmacher. Elmsford, NY: Maxwell Reprint Co., 1970. (Originally published by W.W. Norton & Co., NY, 1938).

_____ . Birth control through the ages. New York: Planned Parenthood/World Population, 1940.

_____ . Birth control: what it is; how it works; what it will do. The Proceedings of the First American Birth Control Conference, New York, NY, Nov. 1921: New York: The Birth Control Review.

_____ . A case for birth control. New York: Modern Art Printing Co., 1917.

_____ . Happiness in marriage. New York: Brentano's 1929.

_____ . Motherhood in bondage. New York: Brentano's, 1928.

_____ . My fight for birth control. Elmsford, NY: Maxwell Reprint Co., 1969. c. 1931.

_____ . The new motherhood. London: Jonathan Cape, 1922.

_____ . The pivot of civilization. New York: Brentano's, 1922.

_____ . The practice of contraception. Baltimore, MD: Williams & Wilkins, 1931.

_____ . "The right to one's body," pp. 517-521; "My fight for birth control," pp. 522-532; "Birth control—A parent's problem or woman's?"; pp. 533-536. In, Rossi, Alice, ed. The feminist papers: from Adams to de Beauvoir. New York: Columbia University Press, 1973.

_____ . Sixth International Neo-Malthusian and Birth Control Conference, March 29, 1925, New York City, New York: American Birth Control League, 1925 & 1926. Volumes I thru IV.

_____ . What every girl should know. London: Jonathan Cape, 1922.

_____ . "Woman rebel." Reprint edited by Alex Baskin: Margaret Sanger, the "Woman Rebel" and the rise of the birth control movement in the United States. Stony Brook, NY: Archives of Social History, 1976.

Margaret Sanger as subject.*

Gray, Madeline. Margaret Sanger: champion of birth control. New York: Richard Marek, 1979.

Reed, James. From private vice to public virtue: the birth control movement and American society since 1930. New York: Basic Books, 1978.

Gordon, Linda. Woman's body, woman's right: a social history of birth control in America. New York: Grossman, 1976.

Kennedy, David M. Birth control in America: the career of Margaret Sanger. New Haven: Yale University Press, 1970.

Coigney, Virginia. Margaret Sanger; rebel with a cause. Garden City, NY: Doubleday, 1969.

Douglas, Emily Taft. Margaret Sanger: pioneer of the future. New York: Holt, Rinehart and Winston, 1969, c1970.

Lader, Lawrence and Meltzer, Milton. Margaret Sanger; pioneer of birth control. New York: Crowell, 1969.

Sanger, Alexander Campbell. Margaret Sanger; the early years, 1910-1917. B.A. Thesis, Princeton University, April 1, 1969.

Lader, Lawrence. The Margaret Sanger story and the fight for birth control. Garden City, NY: Doubleday, 1955.

*Arranged chronologically

# Credits

Edited by

Jessica Miller


Designed by

Hanover Studio Inc.
Harry Chester, Inc.